Rooted & Rising

*A Journey Through Truth,
Love, Beauty, and Justice*

by Elyse Farwell

Rooted & Rising: A Journey Through Truth, Love, Beauty, and Justice
© 2026 Elyse Farwell
ISBN: 978-1-966337-35-5

Cover art: Kelly Eichberger, 2025
First Edition, 2026

All rights reserved. No part of this publication may be reproduced, distributed, or transmitted in any form or by any means, including photocopying, recording, or other electronic or mechanical methods, without the prior written permission of the publisher, except in the case of brief quotations embodied in critical reviews and certain other noncommercial uses permitted by copyright law.

Printed in the United States of America

Edited by: Kappa Curran
Cover Design by: **Kelly Eichberger**
Layout Design by: Jim Dodson

To all the love in my life, and for all the love in the world.

Acknowledgments

I offer deep gratitude for my journey through therapy, which helped me heal and reclaim my voice;

to my dear poets in the San Diego cohort of the Community Literature Initiative, who walked alongside me in creative courage;

and to my beloved family and community of friends, who have always held space for me to show up fully and authentically.

Thank you for encouraging me to speak boldly, live bravely, and write truthfully.

Contents

Acknowledgments ix

Truth 1
   pathways 3
   self love 4
   good girl 6
   anxious attachment 8
   responsibility 9
   compass 10
   called to teach 11
   vessel 12
   welcome home 14
   a call to prayer 16
   enough 17

Love 19
   rain 21
   vulnerability 22
   craving 24
   lost love 26
   moving on 28
   foundation 29
   secure attachment 30
   first love 31
   manifest 32
   dreaming 34
   this time 35
   avoidance 36

Beauty 39
   advent 41
   seasons 42
   renaissance 43
   presence 44
   religion 45
   discovery 46
   strangers 47
   anniversary 48

Justice **51**
   productivity 53
   capacity 54
   state of the union 55
   womanhood 56
   burning 58
   uncivilized 59
   foreigner 60
   deterrence 61
   in times of war 62
   common unity 63
   endangered species 64

"what a privilege it is to grow into the finest version of myself"

-Rupi Kaur, *Home Body*

Rooted & Rising

A *Journey Through Truth, Love, Beauty, and Justice*

Truth

pathways

Inspiration comes at the most
unexpected times.

Much like life and the way it
hits you, knocks the breath right out
of your chest.

So much can change in a
moment's notice, and all of a sudden
you're on a completely different
path.

self love

I have been searching
for far too long,
and I didn't know for what until
I come face-to-face with
myself.

I breathe a sigh of relief.

She is comfortable
in her skin,
in her body,
in her soul.

Hair short, curly, and wild,
a soft smile of
peace and harmony;
calm washes over me.

I found her.

She speaks in a voice that is familiar
and yet unrecognizable.
You have arrived
at who you were always meant to be,
the one that has lived within you
aching to be set free.

I have been waiting for you.

We sit together in this space
meeting each other's gaze, understanding
I am no longer my heaviest burden.
The weight has been lifted,
my own light I have been gifted
after believing I had none;
the shadows are finally gone.

All this time I never knew that I deserve
to protect what is sacred,
to celebrate what is achieved,
to love all of me.

I am worthy.

Self-doubt surrenders.
You're resilient, remember?
How could I forget?

Now sitting alone,
I've always been on my own,
but this time, I am home.

good girl

"You're so nice,"
they tell me,
but they don't realize
there's more than meets the eye.

"Nice" comes from thirty years
of not understanding myself and being misunderstood.
Of not expressing myself
because I didn't know how.

Of being the quiet one,
my silence a mask for the anxiety
that was always simmering
below the surface of a smile.

Of being a follower,
because I didn't trust myself to lead.

It was easier being invisible.

Thirty years
of needing help and
not knowing how to ask for it.

Feeling powerless,
breaking my own boundaries
rather than face confrontation
and risking rejection.

Of craving connection and
not knowing how to reach for it,
fearing the loss of relationships that
I never even had in the first place.

Vulnerability blocked by
decades of building walls,
bricks made out of my own shame.

Thirty years of good girl:
a label revered by society,
a label given to me,
a label I perpetuated within myself.

Only a fraction of who I am,
but I allowed to become my entire being.

I am more than meets the eye;
instead of "nice," try

thoughtful
patient
wise
passionate
vibrant

living life out loud

imperfect
but desirable
and lovable
anyway.

Not a good girl,
but a complete, complex, empowered
woman.

anxious attachment

I am anxiously attached to change.
I crave it, and yet avoid it

at all costs.

Sometimes it's just too hard to let go,
and other times it's an open window,
an invitation to uncover.

So used to moving from place
to place, now I long
for faces that aren't mine anymore.

Change is unpredictable.

Like an anchor, my heart
ties me down
but my feet keep sailing
toward the shore.

Like the sea, and the world spinning
round, change is impossible to control.

responsibility

Envy
has felt all consuming
lately.

I'll have what she's having!
When is it my turn?
Why is everyone else happy but

me?

Envy
is the epitome of
insecurity,

but perhaps also the driving force
of getting unstuck,
climbing out of that rut.

I am responsible for
my own life.

compass

My style is anxiously attached.
My style is a nervous laugh.
My style is insecurity,

but confidently.

My style is vulnerability.
My style is making you feel seen.
My style is listening,

but deafening.

My style is wearing my heart on my sleeve.
My style is standing up for what I believe.
My style is meeting others with compassion,

and taking action.

My style is kindness,
but righteous.

My style is my compass.

called to teach

To be a teacher
is to be many things,
but above all
caring,

and I care a lot.
Too much perhaps,
so much that I have been
lost.

Who am I
if not a teacher?
It's been so long that I almost
forgot.

vessel

Eyes,
my favorite part of me,
azure blue with a hint of green.

Oh, the things they have seen!
Sunrises and sunsets,
mountains and oceans,
nightmares and dreams.

Jaw,
clamped shut for so long
it is rusted and restrained,
chained to my shame.

Slowly released through gritted teeth that
turn into a smile as I honed my craft
and learned to laugh,

let another language open up worlds
and parts of me that I had never known.

Shoulders,
carrying the weight of my world;
tense.
Moving with my every breath,
hunched and slouched, concealing
how I really feel inside.

Relishing the moments when I
pull them back,
standing tall and knocking down
stubborn walls.

Heart,
beating unceasingly,
even when everything is unraveling
it tells me, "I can carry this for you."

Healing and
finally feeling seen,
there's room to bleed
and breathe.

Hands,
clasped in my lap,
nervously picking at fingernails.
They made me feel unworthy
even when they touched
piano keys as I played,
pencils on paper as I wrote,
water as I swam.

Now my confidants reaching
for strength and creativity,
carefully molding the next
version of me.

Feet,
carrying me forward even
when it feels impossible, and
helping me walk away from what
is not meant for me.

They keep me grounded, rooted,
and dancing like no one's watching.

welcome home

Here lies your forever home,
although you wouldn't know it just from
the outside.
It's been left in good condition, relatively untouched.
Don't get me wrong,
people have come and gone.
It's been strained, seen some struggle,

but look at the trees that tower over it,
providing privacy. A sanctuary.
It is a solitary shelter,
a fortress perched on its cliff – vulnerable,
but rising high above the tumultuous sea – unwavering.
The perfect escape.

Go ahead, ring the bell!
A gentle chime is how the inhabitants can tell
someone wants in.
The door opens slowly, unsure at first,
but give it time and you'll see
it's quiet, simple, and serene.

Very few have had the privilege of crossing this threshold,
but there is a large window in the front that begs for the morning
light to intrude,
a pathway ready and waiting for the next adventure,
a porch swing where many have sat to take in the sunset,
and the afternoon breeze renewing depleted spirits,
fresh air bringing hints of faraway lands.
Take in the view,
this expansive ocean right in front of you.

What's in that room there?

That is not ready to be shared.
It's off-limits,
until there's a confirmed commitment.
Genuine interest has been intermittent.
There have not been many with the patience needed
to see beyond the walls
and the flaws.

The thing is, it's never needed anyone really
to stay standing, steadfast,
always lurching fearlessly on the edge,

but consider that it might be lonely.
It's not above unconditional love.
Can you be trusted to cherish it as your own?

If so, welcome home.

a call to prayer

I once was taught to turn away from sin and be faithful to the
gospel.

Now I know that those sins were only mistakes,
choices I made because I didn't know
any better.

Let my experiences be lessons.

I once was convinced that my body is a temple,
not for me but for my
purity.

Now I know my body is an altar,
and I lay acceptance at my feet.

Let self-love be my offering.

I once was baptized with water,
a sacrament that immersed me in shame,
left me with all the blame for being human.

Now I baptize myself with my own words;
my truth, my healing.

Let my voice be all the cleansing I need.

enough

I choose me because

I am not too much;
I am just enough.

I am love.

Love

rain

I've waited for too long.
Why?
It's time.

Unsure,
fumbling,
grasping;

uncomfortable yet enlightening.

Soft,
sweet
release.

I am fine.

The time washes away with the rain

vulnerability

We met.
Just a photo and a conversation
without any words actually being spoken.
Trying to be open,
commonalities are only seeds hoping to
bloom into a flower.

Where do we go from here?

And there you are,
insecurity.
Just as the seed starts to sprout, the
ugly weed breaks through
the skin that I fought so hard to toughen.
Slowly suffocating, withering away.

Am I enough?

Fear always lurking around
every turned corner.
I face you, I overcome you, and
yet here you are again with each
new experience.

Why can't I escape?

Independence, I am
on my own.
I've been here before,
time and again – I don't need anyone
to rescue me.
I am my knight in shining armor,
a rose cutting down its own thorny branches that have guarded
this heart
for too long.

Radiant light seeps in, giving me
the strength I need.
I surrender and I am freed.

Liberation, the weeds may try to
strangle my leaves, my petals;
but here I remain firmly rooted and rising,
they no longer have power over me.
The sun has pierced through the shadows
and given me new life.
I am blooming, welcoming the light.

Don't ever again mistake my vulnerability
as a deficiency.
It is my vitality.

craving

I haven't heard from you, again.
I don't know if it's what you intend –
or if it is just characteristic of how little
you care –
but I need you to be a little more aware,
that as more and more time goes by,
the more I crave you anyway.

Eyes that I barely remember,
from too many missed opportunities for
true connection.
We exchange cautious glances to make sure we're here,
that all of this is real.
Are you afraid of letting me see your soul,
are you more afraid of having to
acknowledge mine?
Your eyes – I crave their gaze.

Hair that is not necessarily memorable,
until I recall the texture of it on
my fingertips –
all of those times that I grasped on to anchor myself to you
as I was gently coaxed into giving in and letting loose.
Are you afraid of pulling your own fingers through my curls,
getting too tangled up in me?
Your hair – I crave its softness.

Hands that have been where
none have before,
tracing patterns on my skin that are familiar, and exhilarating.
After leaving a trail of fire behind, you'll reach out to hold
my own hand in yours and call it
quality time.
Are you afraid of the possibility that someday
soon, I won't release my grip and let you move on?
Your hands – I crave their touch.

Elbows that frame either side of me
like magnets that draw my hands across
your back;
your shoulders and arms,
muscles that contract when I finally grab on,
bracing myself to come undone.
Are you afraid that if you don't maintain the
distance, you'll lose yourself in me?
Your elbows – I crave their security.

Spine that cautiously closes the space between us,
like ocean waves crawling toward the shore.
The rolling rhythm, slow swelling, deafening crash –
the ebb and flow building until our walls collapse.
Are you afraid that this bond will become a
burden too heavy for you to bear?
Your spine – I crave its weight.

Lips that are soft, sometimes smoky, with
hints of desperation and desire –
at first hungry but gentle – they
excite and reassure.
Eventually – limited and indifferent – they confuse and disappoint.
Are you afraid that if they
linger, this becomes more than you were looking for?
Your lips – I crave their taste.

lost love

So exhausted but can't sleep
thinking of you,
filled with so much love for you,
feeling empty from the loss of you
and what we had.

Just like your side of my bed,
this sacred space
once full of us,
the most intimate and vulnerable parts of
you and me
shared between the sheets;

a dream.

Then I turn over
and I'm reminded that you're gone.

How can I move on,

when the one who broke me is the same one
whose arms I want around me
to put me back together again,
rub the small of my back,
smooth my hair,
and tell me everything is going to be alright?

There's too much dark in this
loneliness. I miss your light,
your presence in my life.

You've shown me what love is,
making me feel
seen;
a happiness I didn't know existed
just for me,

until you set me free.

It wasn't our time.
It isn't your fault.
You wanted to give me it all,

but you couldn't –
and you wouldn't –
keep me from a love that's destined to be great.

One thing is for sure:
I have been touched by you
and I will never be the same again.

moving on

I thought you were my person,
so it's hard to let you go.
Then I realize

the only time I knew how you truly felt
was when you weren't afraid of losing me
anymore.

Fear will hold you back,
but love will always push me forward.
I guess I just haven't found my person

yet.

foundation

Run toward
or away?

Love is a choice;
trust will determine which one
you make.

secure attachment

You saw me before anyone else did,
and you embraced all of it.

Giving me peace of mind as I
spiraled, cried, and
lost my way.

Providing a safe space for
vulnerability, curiosity, and
revelation.

Celebrating what it means to be a woman,
the embodiment of another kind of relationship I crave and deserve.

There is nothing like sisterhood.

first love

I knew I was in love when
I felt safe in
your hands.

I knew I was in love when
we could lay in silence and time
still went by too fast.

I knew I was in love when
I could be myself and feel beautiful in
every way.

I knew I was in love when
you reminded me to breathe and everything was okay.

I knew I was in love when
you looked into my eyes and I felt seen for the first time.

I knew I was in love when
we could make each other laugh even as
we cried.

I knew I was in love when
you called just to
say hello.

I knew I was in love when
you felt like
home.

manifest

I found home in you
when you made me smile
and brought a whole new meaning to
quality time.

Taking in the view,
the same mountaintops and cityscapes,
but everything feels new with you.

Exploring good food like we do our bodies,
full of each other but never quite getting enough.

Even when it gets tough,
listening to your heartbeat and
feeling you breathe,
I am at peace.

Strolling down the street,
my head on your shoulder and
we're holding hands,

Enjoying each other's company
whether or not we have any plans.

Lying in the grass, soaking up the sun
or sleeping beneath the stars,
I feel secure in your arms.

Traveling to new places and
meeting new faces that mean something,
falling for you more than I ever knew I would.

Sharing our insecurities, fears, aspirations;
deep conversations

and laughter,
yours a sound I will never forget.

There's nothing we've been through that I regret, every moment with you is fun.

Loving you has been one of the easiest things
I've ever done.

dreaming

Holding each other tight,
if only we could stop time,
tattoo this moment in our minds.

I can still picture the candlelight,
how you made my curves feel like
your own paradise.

Eyes hungry with yearning,
my porcelain skin burning,
waiting for your touch.

Making love to you,
becoming one out of two.

Feeling desired.
Hearts on fire.

Slow kisses,
gentle caresses;
a different kind of purity
with the one who loves me.

Limbs wrapped completely around
each other, skin-to-skin.
There is no place where I end and you begin,

and no place I'd rather be.

You and I are my favorite dream.

this time

I wanted more with you.
I wanted to build a life with you,
to find a house and live the
day-to-day with you,

doing the mundane together and
knowing I'd get to come home to you.

I guess this is what happens when
it's not aligned, trying to combine
two experiences,
two lives,
two minds,

and navigating the challenge of
not seeing eye-to-eye.

I hoped it would be different
this time.
We didn't want to let another opportunity
to have this love pass us by,

and I have no regrets, but I see now
that you just got tired of
trying.

avoidance

I opened my heart
and asked you to do the same.

You said,
"I can't,"
when what you should have said is,
"I won't."

I hope you find whatever it is
you're looking for.

Beauty

advent

Simplicity

routine
balcony
reading
writing
conversation

Nourishment

strength
movement
sun
wind
waves

Resilience

solitude
wallowing
stillness
patience
reflection

Experience

driving
music
laughter
voice
touch

Connection

kindness
compassion
openness
truth
love

Gratitude

seasons

Here's to seasons:
let them be lessons.
Ups and downs,
not at all linear –
and not at all desired timing –
but essential nonetheless.

People come into your life for a reason.

Seasons
of makeups and breakups,
reparations and ruptures,
each one asking us to let go
of a piece of ourselves.
Make room for something new.

Growth leads to a different point of view.

Seasons
of loneliness and connection;
the ebb and flow of fulfillment.
Surrounded by community,
or sitting quiet – just me –
both an opportunity

to learn what love means.

renaissance

This is our golden hour,
transitioning from one era to another.
Time begins ticking away again,

counting all those days that passed us by without
the ones, the things, the routines
we love.

Finally,
glimpses of each other's faces,

an awakening
from too much time sitting and thinking in our own bodies.
We rediscover ourselves and the value of
self-expression and connection,
this shared experience reminding us
what it means to be
human.

Reconstruction manifests in reunions;
to be touched is something we will never take for granted again.
Holding hands,
embracing,
kissing as if we are making up for time lost,

love lost.
Recognizing mortality's cost,
we take advantage of every moment,
rebuilding the ones that were stolen.

The streets are suddenly teeming,
a feeling both welcome and overwhelming.
People chattering,
children laughing,
life's soundtrack following us again everywhere we go.

What will we take with us to our new normal?
Never forget to always stop and smell
the roses.

presence

As you grow older,
how do you return to fun?

Take time to
bask in the sun.

Blast your favorite music on the road
with the windows rolled down.

Stop on your walk just to watch
water cascade down a fountain.

Swim laps and relish
the smell of chlorine on your skin.

Smile when a child hands you a
freshly-picked wildflower.

Notice tiny crystal rainbows appear
on your walls at golden hour.

Sing with friends
around a bonfire.

Don't worry about what's past
or present.

Simply live
moment-by-moment.

religion

Baptism.

Waves crashing,
tide receding on the sand,
toes digging in,
water caressing my skin;
bathing in natural beauty.

Scent of renewal from the first rain
tapping on the windowpane,
pounding on the roof,
reminding me that crying is okay;
washing it all away.

Worship.

Sun-kissed closed eyelids,
the rising and setting a constant,
reminding me to smile.

Moon and stars,
Orion my compass,
navigating sudden changes in direction;
a reminder to find the light in the dark.

Communion.

Trees swaying,
leaves rustling,
hair being tousled in the wind,
and the smell of fresh pine;
fresh air filling my lungs
and my soul.

Heart beating,
birds chirping,
and in the distance,
silence.

My world spins on.

discovery

There is nothing quite like being in
foreign places.
Chance encounters and new faces,
making space for shifting perspectives.

What might I see?
Who might I meet?

Openness is the enemy of prejudice
and a portal to myself.

There is still so much to be discovered.
I look for it in the swirling leaves falling from
swaying trees,

my favorite melody.

Chilled air filling my lungs and bringing
life to my cheeks,
the world spinning more slowly.

Every step outside an opportunity
to strip off more layers, revealing
the best version of me.

I can be whoever I want to be,
and when confronted with curiosity,
the result is that I become
boldly and courageously free.

strangers

You are not really a stranger, are you?
We are just people after all,
sharing the human experience:
love,
loss,
uncertainty and
hope.

If only someone would teach us
to reach out to each other,
hands and hearts opening;
an offering.

We are all so much more connected
than we know.

anniversary

In this tender moment
old wounds open.
The anniversary approaches.

We have been here for so long
waiting,
wishing,
withering.
The light is at the end of the tunnel.

Will we make it before it collapses?

Trying to surrender to the process,
looking for a window,
some insight into how all of this will turn out.

Will we make it out alive?

My breath reminds me that I survived,
that I am a seed.
The sun may feel far away for now,
but as soon as it shines upon me,
I will regenerate.

My value is no longer tied to the waiting.
I am on my own timeline,
and when I am ready, I will know.

Trust:
it is the wisdom I have gathered
during this time.

Justice

productivity

I want to spend my days dreaming, but instead I am just a cog in the capitalist machine. They tell us to work, do, produce, and think, but never to hope or believe in what could be. They keep us in this vicious cycle so we will never have time to break it. I want to tear it down and turn this world back around. I want to feel my toes digging into the ground, into the dirt and sand. I want to feel the leaves and grass on my hand. I want the sun to kiss my eyelids and the rain to fill the silence. I want to share a laugh and a smile, and take time to get away for a little while. I want to see the world – no, not see it – experience it. I want to be a part of something bigger than this.

capacity

If I could make one difference in the world,
I would make more space.

For each of us to have the capacity to live a
full life –
not just survive,
not just scrape by,
but thrive.

To travel the world and
find peace of mind,
truly leave the troubles of the day-to-day
behind.

To not have to worry so much about
money
and still be able to afford
to explore.

Slow down and sit with gratitude,
without constant pressure to have
more.

Time to take care of ourselves and
each other;
to reflect and recognize when we deserve better.

If only we were given the capacity to live
our full humanity.

state of the union

How did we get here?

Year after year,
filled with so much fear,
and with everything on the line.

Feeling out of my mind –
I know logically I'll be fine,
that our country will heal in time,

but these are our rights,

and they'll continue stripping them away.
What's it gonna take
for people to finally get what's at stake?

The Declaration states
that whenever the government becomes
destructive to these ends,
it is the right of the people to defend

Life, Liberty, and the Pursuit of Happiness
for all.

Today we grieve,
tomorrow we get ready
for battle.

womanhood

What does it mean to be a woman?
We are not so easily defined,
but look around and you'll see them try
to confine us to a box
closed in on all sides.

Everyday patronized:
too thick,
too thin,
too much
(but not enough),
too soft,
too strong,

poked, prodded, and trampled on.
Breathless, dizzy,
discomfort, and pain;
you'll feel a little pinch –

suck it up and hold it in.

Sometimes my body
doesn't feel like it belongs to me.
Policy after policy,
my voice –
my choice –
disregarded by men
who don't know what it is to live in this frame,
but will do everything they can to
touch it
and control it anyway.

Lie with us,
lie about us,
shame us into silence,
then tell us what we can and can't do
with none of their own consequences.

This may be a man's world,
but they wouldn't even be here
if we weren't around,
picking up after their messes since the
first ultrasound.

This is my body, not their battleground.

burning

The world is on fire.
Somebody, please make it stop!
When will the smoke clear?

uncivilized

I woke up to take a walk
through the ruins. An ancient city,
only some of it uncovered by slow discovery.

I sat and listened
to the sounds of the jungle coming alive,
uncivilized

and therefore untainted.
The beauty of the third world;
poverty and crime brought about by being

colonized
cannot break the spirit
of a people so full of warmth and tradition.

Sacred rituals bring peace
near polluted waters and cobblestoned streets.

I found myself among
vibrant facades filling my world with color
again.

foreigner

I landed in Ecuador,
had no idea what was in store.

Adapting to a new culture,
exposure
to cloud forests and volcanoes,
rainy season pounding on my windows.
Weekdays spent teaching writing and reading,
going to markets and climbing mountains on the weekend.

¡Que rica la vida!

Until the machismo got to me.

deterrence

Exclusion and entitlement,
a legacy of hostility.

Who gets to decide that someone is
"other?"

Exchanging one fear for another,
they traverse through unimaginable terrain
just to find their way home;
stolen land.

We have been migrating since the
dawn of time.

When did it become a crime?

Surveillance and zero-tolerance
policies that only serve to separate us.

When did it become a crime?

Hostility.
Policies that only serve to separate us.
Exclusion and entitlement
are the death of us.

in times of war

There are no winners in war,
only survivors.

Loss of normal.
Loss of home.
Loss of life.
Loss of love,

buried beneath the rubble
left behind by cowards with
too much power.

So selfish and self-involved,
they have no qualms about pushing buttons
and watching whole cities fall.

From oceans away they claim it's in the name
of justice,
blinded by their own prejudices.
No mercy,

void of empathy.
We fight,
and we fight,
and we fight,
no end in sight.

History is bound to be repeated when
we are none the wiser.

There are no winners in war,
only survivors.

common unity

Since when is codependency a bad thing?
If these last few years have taught us anything,

we need each other more than we know.

Independence, in my experience,
leads to isolation.

Don't get me wrong,
there is something beautiful about
knowing how to be
alone,

but being alone and being lonely
are not one in the same.

When the world is going up in flames
around me,
what I need more than anything is to find
common unity.

endangered species

In the world of adulting,
Santa Claus is an endangered species.
Like a field of poppies, our imaginations
used to be in full bloom.

Summers were spent selling lemonade
and eating banana splits,
splashing in babbling brooks
until the sky was the color of salmon.

Playing make-believe was second nature,
and the world was full of the promise
of infinite dreams.

Then we get older and our elders
call our bluff, tell us we need to "grow up."

Our rough around the edges becomes
polished stone. Reality like sandpaper
rubbing away our unique shapes
until all we see are just reflections.

Our natural state turned into particles
lost to the wind. Like smoke and ash,
they choke out the innocence,
Our most precious pieces.

We spend a lifetime in a blizzard
trying to find our way to
ourselves.

Take me back to a childhood of smooth sailing.

Publisher's Note

Daxson publishing was created to help marginalized artists and their allies publish their work, so the world can hear their voice. The vision for this publishing house is to help people get their work out there, and not have them struggle finding their way through the publishing process. Everyone's voice deserves to be heard, and we are here to help. If you are interested in submitting a manuscript, email daxsonpublishing@gmail.com. Support our cause! Buy our books at daxsonpublishing.com.

www.ingramcontent.com/pod-product-compliance
Lightning Source LLC
LaVergne TN
LVHW050029080526
838202LV00070B/6976